Looking after
Cats
Kittens and

Katherine Starke

Designed by Michael Hill
Edited by Sarah Khan
Illustrations by Christyan Fox

Consultant: Amanda Thomas

Usborne Quicklinks

For links to carefully chosen websites where you can
find out more about cats and kittens, go to the Usborne
Quicklinks website at www.usborne-quicklinks.com
and enter the keywords **"pet guides cats"**

There you'll find links to websites where you can:

- discover the right pet for you
- find fun things to make for your cat
- watch video clips of how to care for cats

We recommend that young children are supervised while on
the internet and follow the safety guidelines displayed on
the Usborne Quicklinks Website. Usborne Publishing is not
responsible for the content of external websites.

Contents

Choosing a kitten

If you are thinking of getting your first cat, it's a good idea to get a kitten. A kitten needs more care to start with but will find it easier to fit into a new home.

Where to start

Ask friends if they know anyone whose cat has had kittens. Local vets and animal shelters are good places to ask too.

If you get two kittens they will keep each other company.

Types of cat

Some people breed cats so that they have certain mixtures of fur colours and length. These cats are described as purebreds or pedigrees. Most cats are a mixture of breeds.

This grey and white kitten is a mixture of different breeds.

This kitten belongs to a breed known as Siamese.

Nearly all ginger cats, like this one, are male.

Which one?

Find out about the kitten's parents if you can. If they seem healthy and well cared for, the kitten probably will be too.

A kitten might grow up to look like its mother or father.

A fluffy cat will probably have kittens that will grow up to be fluffy too.

Try to watch the kittens while they are playing with each other to find out what they are like. Some kittens are quiet and others are more active.

A quiet kitten can take longer to get used to its new home. An active kitten might need to be played with often.

Choose a kitten that's lively but not aggressive. Ask the owners if they have noticed how your kitten behaves.

Play with the kittens before you choose one.

Wild things

Tame cats are called domestic cats. Domestic cats are related to wild cats such as lions, cheetahs and leopards. A lively cat may behave like a wild cat at times.

This kitten is pretending to hunt, like its wild cat relatives.

What will I need?

The next few pages tell you about some of the things you will need for your cat. Make sure you have everything ready before it arrives.

Pet carrier

You will need a pet-carrying box to take your cat home. A normal cardboard box is not safe or strong enough.

Buy a carrier from a vet or pet store.

Food

Buy a few cans or pouches of kitten food for a kitten, or cat food for a cat. Make sure the food has the word "complete" on the label.

Pets always need fresh drinking water. Cats that eat mainly dry food will drink more often.

Use food dishes with shallow sides so that your cat can reach inside.

Litter tray

Inside your house, your cat will need to go to the toilet in a litter tray. Buy a plastic tray and some special grit, called cat litter, to soak up the cat's wee.

Put the litter tray on newspaper to keep the floor clean.

Toys

A cat needs toys so that it doesn't get bored. Never leave your cat with wool, string, or small toys such as bells. It might choke on them.

You can buy cat toys from a pet store, or make your own. (See pages 24-25 for ideas.)

Make a bed

You can buy a bed for your cat from a pet store, or you could make one yourself.

Find a cardboard box, about twice the size of your cat. Cut off any flaps at the top. Carefully cut a section out of one side, about 5cm (2in) from the edges.

Put newspapers in the bottom and around the sides of the box. Fold up an old sweater or blanket. Put this in the bottom of the box to make a comfortable bed.

Put newspapers under the bed to lift it away from the cold floor.

Make sure your cat's bed is in a place
it can get to easily when it needs to.

Just the place

Cats like to have their food
dishes, litter tray and bed
in separate places. Put the
litter tray near an outside
door so your cat knows
which way to go when
it starts going to the
toilet outside.

Try to find quiet places for the cat's food
dishes and bed where it won't be disturbed.

11

First steps

It will take some time for your cat to get used to its new home. Keep it in just one or two rooms for the first few days. Show it its food, litter tray and bed by tapping them gently and calling your cat's name.

Warm welcome

Open the carrying box and let your cat look around. Tip the box very gently so that it can climb out.

Allow your cat to climb out of the box by itself.

Talk to your cat quietly to get it used to your voice.

Let your cat explore its new surroundings without picking it up. If it wants to explore you as well, stay still and let it rub against you.

When it feels at home, your cat may start to wash. This shows that your cat thinks it is in a safe place.

Cats keep clean by licking themselves.

Introducing yourself

Get your cat's attention by calling its name. It is more likely to come to you if you crouch down and are still. If your cat is very shy, speak softly to it and try not to move towards it. Let it come to you.

Your cat could be very nervous and may creep up to you slowly.

Hold out your hands so that your cat can sniff your fingers.

Stroking your cat

Most cats like to be stroked. Stroking may remind your cat of its mother licking it clean. Smooth its fur down gently in the direction that it grows.

Most cats don't like their stomach to be touched, so it's best to avoid that area when stroking your cat.

Stroke your cat gently around its ears and under its chin. Don't touch its eyes, nose or mouth.

Your cat might sit on your lap when it wants to be stroked. If it feels comfortable and happy, it might purr and knead you with its paws. Kittens knead their mother like this when they want milk.

Territory

A cat usually has an area that it treats as its own. This is called its territory. Cats mark things as their territory by scratching them or spraying them with their scent.

Cats often share parts of a territory.

Smells like home

Your cat rubs its head against things to mix its own smell with theirs. This makes places seem less strange to it.

Your cat might rub against furniture...

...and against you, too.

15

Settling in

Most cats enjoy being cuddled and stroked, but make sure your cat knows you are there before you pick it up. Get your kitten used to being handled while it is still young.

Holding your cat

You need to use both hands to lift up your cat. Carefully lift it with one hand under its chest, then gather up its back legs.

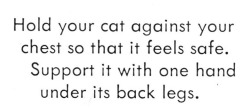

Lift up your cat slowly – never grab it.

Hold your cat against your chest so that it feels safe. Support it with one hand under its back legs.

Talk quietly to your cat to keep it calm.

If it struggles, put your cat onto the floor very gently. Let it go when its feet are on the ground.

Your cat may scratch you if it doesn't want to be held.

The first night

A kitten may feel lonely and miaow a lot when it is left on its own. Wrap a hot water bottle in a towel and put it in its bed for comfort.

Kittens like sleeping snuggled in warm places.

Meeting other pets

It's best to keep other pets away from your new cat for at least two or three days. Never let a cat meet small pets, such as mice, rabbits or birds, that it might think of as food.

The first meetings

Before your pets meet, swap a piece of bedding from each of their beds. This will mix their scents.

Let your pets meet before a meal. They will probably be more interested in their food than each other.

Put their dishes a little distance away from each other.

When two cats meet, they both put their tails straight up. This is a greeting sign.

If your other pet is a dog, keep it on a lead for the first few meetings. Keep the meetings quite short.

Always stay with your pets for the first few meetings.

Joining the family

Have someone with you when your pets first meet so that each pet gets attention. As your pets become used to each other, they will start to feel that they are all part of the same family.

Let both of your pets sniff each other.

Feeding

Cats need to eat meat to stay healthy. In the wild, your cat would eat small animals such as mice, fish and birds. A lot of cats like cows' milk but it can give them an upset stomach, so only give your cat milk occasionally.

Feeding your cat

Loud miaowing might be a sign that your cat is hungry. Feed it at the same times each day.

Your cat might sit by its dish when it is hungry.

MiAOW! MiAOW!

Give a kitten specially formulated kitten food.

While it is up to four months old, feed your kitten four or five small meals a day. This is better than two big meals.

Fill a separate dish with cold water. Make sure there is always fresh water in your cat's dish.

When your kitten is around six months old, start cutting down its meals to two or three a day, but give bigger portions.

Once your cat is around 12 weeks old, you can start ----→ giving it adult cat food.

Cats like to be left alone when they eat.

Keep the dishes in a quiet corner.

Dry foods

Crunching on dry cat food helps to keep your cat's teeth clean. Your cat will drink more water if it's eating dry food. Don't mix dry food with other food or it will get soggy.

As a treat for your cat, you can buy a special ball that gives out dry food as your cat plays with it.

Dish position

Try not to move your cat's dishes around – cats like to eat in the same place every day. If you have two cats, give them separate dishes.

Some dishes have rubber bases, so they don't move easily while being used.

Teeth and tongue

At six months old, kittens lose their first teeth and grow adult ones. Cats' teeth are very sharp and good at biting. Cats don't chew their food as much as people do, but chop it up instead.

MiAOW!

Cats only have a few small teeth for chewing...

...but have longer teeth for biting.

A cat has a rough tongue covered with tiny hooks. The hooks are useful for cleaning fur and, in the wild, for tearing meat off bones.

A cat uses its tongue like a spoon, to lap up water.

Playing

Cats and kittens love to play. They like toys which they can roll and pounce on.

Kittens love climbing on things so they can see all around.

These kittens are playing in a kitten house.

Kittens and cats like to climb inside boxes and paper bags. Keep plastic bags away from your pet, because it could suffocate in one.

Make a playhouse

Making a kitten playhouse is a good way of keeping your pet entertained.

Bend the flaps
out of the box.

Find a cardboard box bigger than your kitten. Make sure the box has four flaps at the top.

Draw one circle
across two flaps.

Draw circles of different sizes on the box. Make some bigger and some smaller than your kitten.

Get someone to help you cut out the circles with a pair of scissors. Tape the flaps together firmly.

Why do cats play?

Cats play mainly to exercise but also
to learn how to hunt. They're also
very inquisitive and like to
explore new things.

A mother cat will
twitch her tail
for her kittens
to chase.

Kitten games

Watch how your kitten plays different games
with its toys. It may pretend it is catching a
bird by throwing a toy up in the air. Kittens of
wild cats do this too, playing with their food.

You can buy balls and toy
animals from a pet store.

26

Watch out for claws

Your kitten might grab you with its claws when you are playing with it. Calm it down by talking to it quietly. Take your hand away slowly.

From time to time, let your cat catch the toy it has been chasing after.

Make sure any hanging parts of your cat's toys are securely attached and can't be pulled off easily.

Fur

Fur protects your cat's skin and helps to keep it warm, just like your clothes protect you. Cats keep their fur clean by licking it with their rough tongues.

Usually cats keep themselves very clean and don't need baths.

Cats can twist to clean every part of their fur.

Keeping cool

In hot weather your cat may wash its fur more often. This is like having a shower to cool down. It may also lie stretched out, so that more air can reach its skin.

Cats stretch out, not only to relax, but also to keep cool.

Shedding

Cats shed some of their fur all the time. Old hairs fall out and are replaced by new ones. Cats' fur grows thicker in winter. In spring, they shed their thick winter fur.

keeping fur healthy

When your cat washes, it swallows loose fur. Swallowing too much can make it sick. You can help your cat to get rid of loose fur by brushing it regularly.

Brush your cat at least once a week. Long-haired cats may need brushing more often.

Cat brushes

Relax your cat by stroking it before you start brushing.

Get an old towel or blanket for your cat to sit on. Sit your cat on your lap or on a table.

Start by brushing its back, then its legs and tail. Brush your cat under its chin and around its ears.

Brush the fur in the direction it grows.

Only brush your cat's stomach if it likes it.

Some cats don't like being brushed at all. Try to get your kitten used to being brushed while it's still young.

Don't brush near its eyes.

Concealing colours

In the wild, cats have fur colours and patterns that match the places where they live. Tigers have stripes which look like the long grass that they hide in to sneak up on their prey.

Domestic cats come in lots of different colours. They don't have to hunt for food, so being able to hide isn't important.

Paws and claws

In the wild, cats use their paws and claws to catch food and to protect themselves. Your cat's paws and claws also help it explore.

A cat uses its claws to dig into things, such as trees and fences, so that it can climb. When it finds a new object, it might tap it with its paws to see if it is safe.

Playing a hunting game, this kitten has caught its "prey" and is digging its claws into it.

Fur between its toes helps a cat walk very quietly, so it can sneak up on its prey.

Scratching signs

A cat scratches against hard surfaces to keep its claws sharp. The scratches also show other cats that it has been there.

Scent glands on your cat's paws leave a smell where ⟶ it scratches.

When it scratches, your cat leaves its smell behind as a sign to mark its territory.

Walk like a cat

Cats swing their paws in front of each other as they walk, as if they are walking along a line. This means that they can easily walk along narrow ledges and fences.

A walking person leaves two lines of footprints.

A walking cat leaves a single line of pawprints.

Scratching posts

All cats need somewhere to scratch. Outside, your kitten will use a tree to sharpen its claws. Inside, if your kitten tries to scratch the furniture, you need to buy a scratching post and train it to use it.

A scratching post has rough rope or carpet around it.

Like this kitten, cats like to stretch up when they scratch.

If you see your kitten scratching the furniture, say "No!" in a firm voice. Take it to its scratching post.

Train your kitten by lifting its paw gently up and down against the post.

All about claws

There are four toes on each of a cat's front paws and one small toe higher up its leg, a bit like a thumb. This is called a dew claw.

A cat's claws are pulled in most of the time to stop them from being worn away too quickly.

Cats put out their claws when they want to scratch.

Litter trays

If your cat is not old enough to go outside by itself or just prefers to stay indoors, it will need to go to the toilet in a litter tray. You might have to train a kitten how to use a litter tray.

Litter tray training

When your kitten has finished eating, pick it up and put it in its litter tray. Leave your kitten to go to the toilet on its own.

Always be gentle when you are picking your kitten up.

Your kitten might forget where its litter tray is at first.

If you see your kitten crouching down with its tail up, pick it up. Quickly take it to its litter tray so that it can go to the toilet.

Empty the litter tray every day. Put the dirty litter into a plastic bag and throw it away. Refill the tray and put it on old newspapers.

Wear rubber gloves and wash your hands after emptying the tray.

Use your kitten's name when you're training it. It will start to recognize its name the more you use it. Praise your kitten when it does something that you want it to.

Keep the tray near an outside door, away from your kitten's food and bed.

yes and no

As your kitten grows up, it will need to learn what it can and can't do in your house. Your kitten will learn faster if you teach it while it's still young.

Saying "yes"

When you're training your kitten and it does what you want it to, praise and stroke it, and give it something to eat as a treat.

Find out which treats your cat like best.

Don't give your cat chocolate or leftovers from your meals. These can make it very ill.

Most cats will like a teaspoon of yogurt or a small piece of cheese as a treat. They may also like a small piece of cooked meat or fish, but remember to pull out all the bones.

Saying "No"

When you see your kitten doing something it shouldn't, say its name and "No!" in a firm voice.

Never shout at or smack your cat.

Your kitten will want to explore. Say "No" if you see it climbing onto surfaces where food is prepared and eaten.

Cat language

Some cats like to miaow a lot to tell you how they feel. You can also watch the way your cat moves to find out what it is saying to you.

Feeling happy

Your cat shows that it's pleased to see you by pointing its tail straight up and its ears forwards. It might also make a chirruping noise to say "Hello".

A cat sways its tail gently when it is happy.

When it is happy, your cat makes a rumbling sound called a purr. It makes the noise deep in its throat as it breathes.

Your cat might arch its back, like this kitten, when it says "Hello".

A cat's back is very flexible — it is made up of twice as many bones as a human's back.

Feeling safe

When your cat rolls over and shows you its stomach, it trusts you. It will probably not do this if there is someone nearby who it doesn't know.

A cat's stomach is a very sensitive area of its body.

Feeling angry

When a cat is angry, it twitches its tail and its ears point back. The black part of its eyes, called the pupils, grow wider. Leave your cat alone if it looks annoyed.

Cats fluff up their fur like this to make them look bigger.

When a cat is angry or scared, it flattens its ears.

It may put its claws out, ready to fight.

An angry cat may also hiss or spit.

Mixed messages

Sometimes, when a cat is playing, it mixes signs that it is happy or angry. It may fluff up its fur but point its ears forwards.

When a cat is playing, its ears might point forwards to show that it's happy, but its fur might fluff up to show anger.

A cat is happy when it is playing, but might be pretending to be angry as part of its game.

You can tell this kitten is playing because it's showing happiness and anger at the same time.

Going to the vet

It's a good idea to take your cat to the vet regularly, even if it is not ill. The vet can check that your cat is healthy.

At twelve weeks old...

...your new kitten should be checked by the vet and given injections to protect it from common cat diseases.

At six months old...

...your kitten can be neutered. This is a small operation which stops it from being able to produce kittens.

Every year...

...your cat will need injections from your vet to make sure it is still protected against diseases.

Emergency visits

If you are worried that your cat is ill, find the number of your nearest vet. Ask the vet for advice before taking your cat in – visiting a vet can be expensive.

While your sick cat is at home, keep a blanket around it if it is lying down, so it feels calm and warm.

Try to stay quiet when you're near an ill cat.

VET'S SURGERY

Leave it in its box until the vet is ready to see you.

To carry your cat to the vet, pick it up carefully and put it into its carrying box. Put it in bottom first, not head first.

Spotting the signs

There are signs you can look out for that may mean your cat needs treatment or special attention from you.

Fleas

If you see your cat scratching a lot, it might have fleas, even if its fur is very clean. Use flea powder or spray to get rid of them.

Fleas can spread, jumping from your cat onto other animals and people.

Tapeworms

If you see something like a grain of rice near its bottom, your cat may have tapeworms living in its stomach. Don't touch them, but tell an adult.

A cat might eat a lot if it has tapeworms.

Getting older

Cats can live for 14 years or longer. As your cat gets older, you might see that it's having problems stretching around to clean its fur.

Older cats will sit and sleep more.

Let your cat sit in a warm, quiet place.

Help your cat keep clean by brushing it more often, particularly in the areas that are hard for it to reach, such as its back and thighs.

Going outside

If you have a garden, your cat can go outside two weeks after it has been vaccinated. Put a cat collar with an identity tag on your cat in case it gets lost.

Make sure you can easily get two fingers under your cat's collar.

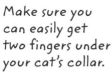

When you want your cat to come inside, call its name or shake a box of cat food.

Crouch down and hold out your hand when you see your cat coming towards you.

RATTLE...
RATTLE...

The right collar

Make sure your cat's collar can open or stretch. It needs to be able to do this so your cat can escape if the collar catches on something.

Check your cat's collar regularly to make sure it hasn't become too small.

An engraved metal tag, like this one, makes your contact details easy to find.

TIBBS
123 CALICO RD . PERTH
PU55 2KT . 555 678910

Indoor space

Some cats prefer to stay indoors. Those cats will still need enough space to exercise inside and a sunny place to sit.

Cat flap training

A cat flap is a small door for your cat. It allows your cat to go outside and come back inside when it likes.

Prop the cat flap open with a ruler or stick. Tempt your cat through it with a food treat or a toy.

After your cat has gone through the flap, go to the other side and tempt it through again.

Try to keep your cat's attention on the toy.

Take away the prop. Push the flap gently to show your cat how it works.

Let your cat push through the flap a few times. Your cat will soon get used to using it.

Make sure the flap is at the right height for your cat.

Some cat flaps have locks on them so that you can keep your cat inside. Don't lock your cat outside at night.

Only leave a cat flap propped open like this when you are training your pet. You don't want other cats coming into your house.

Cat fights

A group of cats may share a territory, but there is always one who is leader. They sometimes fight to see which one that will be.

Play-fighting

As kittens play together, they learn how to defend their territory. Kittens often look as if they are fighting and may even hiss or spit.

Even when kittens are playing, they make themselves look as big and fierce as they can.

Kittens learn how to fight from a young age by practising with their brothers and sisters.

Leadership challenge

If you hear cats making loud wailing noises, they may be challenging each other over which one is the leader. If one of the cats walks away or backs down, then a cat fight is usually avoided.

Whichever cat doesn't back down is the leader.

These play-fighting kittens won't scratch or bite each other hard, so won't get hurt.

Hunting

No matter how well fed your cat is, it may still like to hunt, or play at hunting.

In the dark

In dim light, your cat sees objects five times better than you can.

Good night vision makes it easy for cats to hunt at night without bumping into things.

The animals that cats hunt can't see as well in the dark as they can. Cats also use their whiskers to feel when objects are close.

Getting ready to pounce

When a cat sees something to catch, it stays still then moves slowly closer. Its whiskers and ears point to the front and it watches very carefully. It pounces suddenly.

Perched in a high place, this kitten may wait for a long time to pounce on something.

Pouncing on rolling toys is good practice for hunting.

Cats and plants

You may see your cat nibbling at plants. It's best not to let it eat any plants except grass and a type of herb called catnip or catmint.

The smell of catnip makes most cats very playful. Some cat toys have catnip inside. See pages 58-59 for how to make a catnip toy.

You can grow catnip in any type of soil outdoors, or in a pot indoors.

Eating grass

Some experts say that eating grass helps cats to be sick to get rid of any fur they may have swallowed. If you haven't got a garden, grow some grass in a pot for your cat.

Chewing houseplants

Some houseplants are poisonous to cats. If you see your cat chewing a houseplant, say "No!" firmly. Put pieces of citrus peel in the plant pot – most cats don't like the smell.

Crocus   Hyacinth   Poinsettia

These are some of the houseplants that are poisonous to cats.

Make a catnip toy

Tie some catnip together. Hang it upside-down in a paper bag. Put the bag in a warm, dry place.

Catnip takes about a week to dry.

When the leaves are dry enough to crumble in your fingers, take them out.

Don't make the tail too thin.

Draw a fish shape on some thin paper. Make it about 10cm (4in) long and 5cm (2in) wide.

Pin the fish to some felt. Carefully cut around the shape. Do this twice. Pin the two pieces together.

58

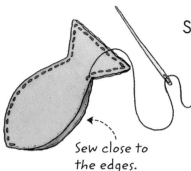

Sew around the edges
using small stitches.
Leave a big gap on
the bottom edge
for the filling.

Sew close to
the edges.

Pull a piece off a cotton
ball and push it into the
fish. Add catnip and
more cotton ball.
Sew up the gap.

Draw on eyes
with a felt-tip pen.

Squeeze the fish to
make the catnip
smell come out.

Going away

If you go away overnight, you need someone to look after your cat. Some cats like to travel but most prefer to stay at home where they feel safe.

Play with your cat and give it lots of attention before you go out.

Cat hotels

When you go away, your cat can stay in a cattery, like a cat hotel. Take your cat's blanket to the cattery. The cattery will provide all the other things it needs.

Your cat's blanket will remind it of your home.

Home comforts

If you decide to leave your cat at home while you are away, ask a friend or neighbour to visit every day to feed your cat and empty its litter tray.

Make sure your friend knows how to call your cat back in.

If your cat is old enough, ask your friend to let it out for a short time. If you have a cat flap, leave it unlocked so that your cat can go out when it likes.

Moving

If you move house, your cat will have to get used to a lot of changes. Packing and moving will seem very strange to it.

Keep your cat inside and let it play in its carrying box for a few days before you move. It will have to stay in the box for the whole of the journey to your new home.

If the journey will be long, choose a carrying box with gaps in the sides so that the cat will be able to see out.

Pack your cat's litter tray, litter, food, dishes and some toys all together just before leaving.

Arriving

When you are ready to leave, put a food treat inside the carrying box and lift your cat into it.

Make sure you put the box containing the cat's things somewhere you can find easily when you arrive.

Your cat will settle more quickly if it has familiar things around it straight away.

When you arrive, let your cat explore its new surroundings. Keep it inside for a couple of weeks, until it has settled in and begun to feel comfortable in its new home.

Give your cat some water and food as soon as you arrive.

Index

Cover design by Kate Rimmer
Additional design by Kathy Ward
Digital manipulation by Keith Furnival

Photo credits

(t-top, m-middle, b-bottom, l-left, r-right)
Cover © Mark Taylor/Warren Photographic; 5ml, 38b, 44r, 52-53 © Mark Taylor/Warren
Photographic; 4b, 5b, 41t, 43b, 47m © Jane Burton/Warren Photographic; 5tr, 7b, 17b, 22t,
28b © Jane Burton & Mark Taylor/Warren Photographic; 9b © Jane Burton; 13b © Jane
Burton/naturepl; 27r © Rob Walls/Alamy; 29m © petographer/Alamy